RAW HONEY

MARIE HARRIS

Printed in the United States of America

Cover painting by Arthur Yanoff

I would like to thank the editors of the following publications
where versions of some of these poems originally appeared:

*Epoch; The Lamp in the Spine; Foxfire; Southern Poetry Review;
Granite; Arion's Dolphin; Stooge; The Ohio Review; Falling
Fountains; Poetry NOW; Shaman; Trellis; Lynx; Truck; 13th Moon;*
BLACKSMITH I (anthology); MOUNTAIN MOVING DAY (Crossing Press
anthology).
HERBAL originally appeared as an issue of *Measure*; Tribal Press;
Bowling Green, Ohio

The publication of this book
was supported in part by a
grant from the National Endowment
for the Arts; Washington, D.C.

Special thanks to New Hampshire Composition, Inc.

Alice James Books are published
by Alice James Poetry Cooperative

ALICE JAMES BOOKS
138 Mount Auburn Street
Cambridge, Massachusetts   02138

CONTENTS

HERBAL

WIVES

RAW HONEY

INTERSTATE

HERBAL

Basil

Plant in average soil. When the small-toothed, ovate,
glossy leaves grow two inches in size, and before
the plant flowers, gather the nesting scorpions from
beneath the leaves and let them sting your hands
and eyes and tongue.

Basil is an antidote for sting of scorpion.

The summer sky is thick with muscle and flight and music
Cygnus, Aquila, Lyra, Hercules
I shrink to the outer rim of my orbit
away from the lashing tail
of the poison constellation

For the muscles in my back, my stomach, the nerves
near Antares, I cut back the plant with my teeth,
like a cat stalking a specific for ache of the heart.

If you will come down from the roof I will make you
an infusion of basil leaves.

Oil of Basil:

to calm the nerves;
to lure scorpions;
to burn the lamps;
to heal bruises;
as a substitute for liquor, tobacco, coffee and sex;
to anoint the corpse;
to use with all tomato dishes;
boiling, to pour on the enemy.

They built a house, but were never happy in it
because they had built it on a spot where basil
did not flourish.

They built a house on ground where basil flourished
and were beset by scorpions every summer.

1

Lemon Balm

*Pliny saith that it is of so great virtue, that though
it be but tied to his sword that hath given the wound,
it stauncheth the blood.*

John Gerard

It is well to plant balm about places where bees are
kept; they find their way home by it.

I never
want to see you again.

And this Peruvian remedy for indigestion:
Toast a slice of bread until it is charred black.
Put the charred bread and some fresh balm leaves into a cup;
add boiling water
and steep for about five minutes.
Pour the liquid off.
That should keep you busy.

The nightmare of having a family.
The nightmare of not having a family.

This harsh lemony herb
is probably as effective as anything
against the biting of mad dogs.

If I were a witch and you came to me late at night and furtive,
I might give you wine with lemon balm against the night and
terror and the throbbing of your gums; I might turn you away.

When I had bees swarming in my hair you were afraid
to touch me. Now though, I only have bees in my hair.

Dill

for William and Sebastian

The young cat knew enough to lick her firstborn, but
she didn't know enough to stop.

I trusted nothing
but the boring fists and elbows
my muscles made: that fact
and the facts of William and Sebastian Matthews.
My instincts ran to violence, ocelots
on leather leashes,
untrustworthy.

It was learning another way to walk, one hand
in front of the other.

My neighbors grow acres of Romilar,
Enfamil, Kaopectate, A&D Ointment,
Pampers, paregoric,
St. Joseph's

and I grow dill because it stalks the garden
taller than anything
and the split seeds stain my fingernails.
Dill water. For hiccoughs.
For sleep.
You two will drink anything
believing it's my strange lullaby
and I love you.

Sage

Why should a man die whilst sage grows in his garden?
Sage masks the odor of meat kept too long past winter

takes away shaking of the members

when I was eight I fell
off a steamshovel
I have been afraid of something
ever since

It is likewise commended against the spitting of blood

I virtually never spit blood

strengtheneth the sinews

while I am dying
I pass time
honing my forearms
to the tension of milkweed pods
I am stronger than he thinks
but I have no idea how strong I am

4

Parsley

I can't get past the border
the beginning
edges of everything catch
at the corners of my eyelids.
This indecision
is called being only
at the parsley and rue.

She is in need of parsley;
she is dying.

plain or flat leaved, fern leaved,
moss leaved, Hamburg
or parsnip rooted:
we are all dying alone
and there is so much left
to do together.

Parsley makes a simple green soup.

It is unlucky to transplant parsley
so I am leaving
or
so I am coming home.

Rue

I will make food for you.

A paste
of the leaves of rue
stamped together with figs or walnuts
is good against all evil airs

perhaps we could talk
in a common language   Greek
for instance

a twelve-penny weight of the seed
drunk in wine
is a counterpoison insomuch
that when the weasel is to fight with the serpent
she arms herself
by eating rue
against the might of the serpent

hands of a pianist hands
of a doctor
green with thumbs
everything I am not
rue, when dried, tends to lose its properties

Hang a bunch in the kitchen to ward off flies
and in bed to repel bugs

I am rue   touch me
and your skin
will raise up blisters, welts, and other accidents

perhaps now we can talk

Monkshood

tooke his name of the Greeke word signifying corruption, poison, or death

she pulled me out the kitchen door
to see them
the deadly spring flowers
wonderful
purple

I have been waiting for you all afternoon
shall we take a large dose
and be done with it

Houseleek

Jupiter's beard
hens-and-chickens
sempervivum...
this plant is always green, neither is it hurt
by the cold in the winter, growing in its native soil.

Its juice
takes away the fire of burnings and scaldings
cures gout and deafness
hemorrhage and headache

but it is not for these
that you grow it on your roof,
that its woody stalks and gross leaves
push under the shingles
spread like stars under your bed
like little tongues very curiously minced in the edges,
nor is it to ward off lightning.

Plant one more woman.
She will multiply like chickens,
images of herself, thick and juicy,
and it will not matter what you call her
but that she is there.

Mint

We walked, Cynthia and I,
to an outcropping above the falls
before the mint had started from the ground
and I remembered
that I have begun every spring
that way, chill and waiting,
watching swallow circles below me
the rainbow below me
keeping my eye at the place
where the water scores the cliff until
it is either water falling or the rock
rushing upward.
She talked about balance.

Mint is a present help for those that be bursten inwardly
of some fall received from an high place

"Now for the first time you are not safe
in your old way of life."

Mint defies my tending.
Its persistence, like the Boston Post Road,
makes me tear my hair.

Rosemary

Mary, it is almost possible to forget.
We sit around your kitchen table
with great mugs of tea,
Roberta cursing the sunlight angling off the snow,
Peggy shaking out her new head of hair,
Laurie, earnest   bursts of laughter
and the children sounding as if they belong here
the footsteps of the men are more direct
all of us content to be going nowhere much
this morning.

Rosemary comforts the brain, the memory, the inward senses,
and restores speech to them that are possessed with the
dumb palsie...

bunches of herbs hang above your stove
drying for years, too brown to recognize

it's getting easier to forget

"I'll tell you what we talk to ourselves about.
We talk about our world. In fact we maintain
our world with our internal talk."

It's time we were up and about, Mary.
The news is getting stale
like breadcrumbs marking where we've been.

Tarragon

The seed of flax put in a radish root or sea onion,
and so set, brings forth the herb tarragon.

It is unlikely
that I will ever come this way again
tin hat
Johnny Appleseed of tears

One Saturday Miss Bird
let me out of the children's section of the town library
and it has come to this

Seldom produces seeds

If tarragon hasn't lasted this winter
frost and ice heaving the roots to the surface
of the bruised ground
then that's that

The sleeper dreams she is asleep.
Her eyes are heavy with the pressure
of the snow tide.

WIVES

The Wind's Wife

Children stamp on it, and men in mockery call it
'The wind's wife'. It is a condition, a sickness,
a loneliness that results in low wages and merits
the smug smile of the car mechanic. But there is nothing
that is, by its nature, lonely, except perhaps the black
widow who can count on visitors, which, what with spinning
and eating, may be more than sufficient to her needs.
In order to feel the comings and goings along the silk
you must be at the center, there to funnel the wind and
be left by it after the blow.

Fishwife

They thought I was a boy, diving for beach peas
like a brown pelican while they stood, camera hung,
on the rocks. I was what they'd come all this way to see:
the diving boy who never came up. I swallow pennies
and gold rings. I have become shy and impossible to locate.

The Bullfighter's Wife

His wife, certainly, is the bull. And if that's a metaphor,
it's one the bullfighter better not forget. Consider the
bull's position: feet braced, head and horns lowered to
groin level, eyes afraid and angry and the color of tulips.
Soon it will be dead, one way or the other; the bullfighter's
concern is to provide it with a plausible death. There is
a respect accorded the bull in the ring. It is allowed
to make a safe place somewhere in the circle and will be
coaxed out like a schoolchild taunted into tears. The bull
returns to its place until the blood in its eye becomes
the new beacon, the recorded message, the color of
everything, the connector that closes the brain's circuit.
When the bullfighter takes the dangerous position directly
in front of the bull, sword over the horns, it is only
to beg the secret of his own death.

The Shark's Wife

By means of this disc the remora attaches to floating bodies and often rides for considerable distances.

Passing below an anxious whale, she tightens the disc
muscle. She has seen most of what there is to see
of the Barrier Reef, the Indian Ocean, the deserted shallows
near Durban, and she is as restless as a blue haired matron
in January. Her flesh crawls with sharks. Oh, just to let go!
to climb the leg of a wader . . . to pick small crustacean
parasites from the ear of a gull . . . to taste meat.

Seawyf

The yellow larch is shedding to driftwood. She hears
the ocean in the shell of a frying pan. The cat
scratches in sand. The children listen to sea songs
and stories of death. There is salt in the oatmeal and salt
on the ladder . . . A fly lights in her hair. The pump kicks
in. The phone rings. Tomorrow she will learn to build a boat.

My Father's Wife

My father's wife makes orange stitches. She pricks her
finger so many times she cannot go to sleep. Night after
night her teeth fall out of her mouth like nonsense rhymes
and she sings and sings until, with my head cradled in
my hands, I scream for her to stop. I tell her that her babies
will be born with no teeth. I tell her that her teeth
will fall out. I tell her that my teeth need attention.
I tell her The Tale of the Teeth Mother. I rock her in my arms
while her teeth fall out—some fall onto rocky ground
and shrivel and some fall onto thorny ground and are
choked and some fall onto fertile ground to sprout and grow
wings and the teeth lovers fly around her like sharp eyed
birds.

Midwife

I have nothing to tell my beads. Tonight is not longer,
day will not break sooner, the crusted kettle will come
to the boil, the children are fast asleep together in
the same bed, at last. Would you ask that I were not with you,
not here tonight watching your face knot like a sheet? that
I did not turn my face to the window where, in the dark
yard, the rooster rubs black and white feathers off a hen
and the goose sails an unruffled dream in the ragweed
        nothing to tell you   my fingers busy at nothing
but weaving the beaded minutes toward morning

Housewife

On a windless night, the fire quiet in the woodstove,
a rat defines the space between inside and out. Corn
scattered for the geese brings them honking in, brings
jays and juncos, and the rat. The rat is what she hears
nesting in the insulation: it has the run of the place.
It hears her turning in her sleep, tracks the distance
from sink to stove to telephone. She keeps it out, it
keeps her in. They have a certain dread in common.

Alewife

There she is, silver among a million silver travelers,
anonymously silver, uniformly beautiful, silver
and moving: caught: disappearing.

RAW HONEY

Sister Claude

What do the pygmies say to Sister Claude
and how do they imagine she came to be so tall?

When she works in the fish factory she tosses her leather
cross onto her back so as not to catch it in the machinery.

Is there a man in Kenya who would not want Sister Claude
for his wife?

You see, she talks about being married to Christ, The Great
Polygamist, gardener of the family flowers.

The heart of Sister Claude is flexing, growing thick
and strong as a bicep.

The Quilt

The auctioneer turns her. The men wait on a corn planter
and a wooden box of assorted nails. She is offered from
the porch of her own house. We pluck at her skirt. What
is she to me? I am waiting for the box of nails. What
is she to me? The quilt measures five by six feet. There
are ten thousand seven hundred squares, each one quarter
inch square. I try again to think of the neutron star.
I am so angry! How can I think of mass without volume
or imagine the woman of such a quilt.

Luxury Apt

It never gets dark. Crickets suffocate with little clicks
in the air conditioning. Where are the creaking boards,
the window pane that rattles? Light without sun. Airplanes
or buses opening into terminals. There has been a strike
or a storm, some foul-up no one understands though rumors
fly, and we grow roots in our places in line. We are plane
trees chewing concrete, swaying in smoke, blossoming under
fluorescence, watching the cat. And when the cat rolls over
stiff legged and wheezing, we know we have less than an hour
to get out.

Visitors

If you had not heard of the northward migration
of the Brazilian killer bee, loosed inadvertently
by a greedy honey baron, you would have slept that much
easier. It's the way with all pieces of surprising
information. Your life is changed daily and as arbitrarily
as a traffic light, and your marriage lies dormant for
as long as an alligator pear pit on toothpicks. Leave the
food on your plate. Someone will eat it.

Song

Hair
like heather, father would boast,
when my feet were still
soft and my breath
sweet as a calf's.

When the eyes of cows
reproached me, when
the girls swelled for love
of their boys, I left,

learned other skills
and carried the coals
of my efficiency all over
the city. I pleased
more than one man
that way.

Father, my fingers are cold.
I have no heart
or song in this town.
My men go home at night
and I am not pretty

not pretty any more.

Facts of Winter

The thermometer is not to be believed:
facts in winter are noisier than that.
The trees yip like dogs and the wind screeches
one skid after another.
Have you listened
to the frozen apples banging?
Don't shout! The cloud avalanche is massing.
Will you ever forget the winter of '71 . . .
sure, we all have our stories — bursting pipes,
strangers huddled in the Texaco station, electrical
cutbacks, states of emergency, what have you—
but did I tell you how
my friends and I became separated
between here and the barn.

Leaving

Moving, slowly at first
a walk further than usual
earlier than before, though not quite at dawn,
a loose leash of daylilies on the ankle
then a night run under Orion disappearing
each horizon a new mote in the eye
moving along:
is how, looking back,
we leave.

Mushroom Hunting

The ground underfoot is slippery
with leaves
forest kelp
the fertile choke of autumn

you have let me down

I turn the wet pages of the field guide
What I have brought with me will be enough

Payment

The heat's off.
Last year that would have meant
the furnace quit:
flood or failure
to meet payments. I'm not paying
for heat this year
so adjust the thermostat from room to room
open windows indiscriminately
track wind on the carpet.
I dream of little vibrating motors
of money and dreams
churning it out free all free.

Late February

and it breaks again
like the fat cattail

small full minute of peace

breaks
down its length breaks
messily open

party

spring begins slowly in the colors
of old bruises

it's been a long winter, he said,
watching everyone at his party kiss
everyone else every
tongue in every mouth remembering
private moments

we all break
into brittle tears
the best parties end that way

Rita

Death
was dying
was dying a long time
death that they watched
death most mumbling
death by internal drowning
a beached Chevy covered in plastic
ought to bury it with her or burn it
death with almost no body left
dying by ounces while they watched
bag full of dying
cells
like feeding flies
eating death and dying
saying
the dead words

July

you are uneasy in your own house:
you range from room to room to escape
the heat
you remonstrate with the blue velvet sofa
and despise seven chairs in the diningroom
find fault with orange lilies closing
in the kitchen

in the short season of carpenters and plumbers
the season of complaint
sweating with unbearable birdnoise
you open and shut the refrigerator
waiting for winter

landscape

the edges of sky
and ocean grate
without a watery cloud
or whitecap to grease the point of contact

air this sharp
keeps us quiet
it's unwise
(look at the boys throwing
a stick to the dog
swimming out and back
out
and back)
to talk
into this megaphone
of an absolutely clear day

drowning

every day the lake water gets deeper
a white half moon sails like a shark through the clouds
green backed swallows
little boats
dark brown legs moving to keep afloat
in the space between

deep

we can measure this: tie a little clay pot
to a ball of twine .
and drop it into the well

past spiders and snake holes
into the leafy pool

as long as the string is wet
measures

we are at our best when dancing

bread and eggshells rise around us
the dog and cat are drinking from the white bowl
here are the ones
with sense enough to come in out of the rain
and having come in
find there is nothing much to talk about
except the weather
out of the rain again
wet from not coming in soon enough
shifting from foot to foot we take in
our surroundings

the hills settle with a rustle like chickens

not a bat
but the shadow of a bat cast by Jupiter
we duck as from a blow
flinch when the birch branch hits the windshield
start at the echo of a coon hound bounding toward us
across the valley
stand very still by a burdock blind
the late wind raising hairs along our arms

Mother of

(a silence a long silence)
quiet as fern sex
while we determine what order to rescind
the bearing is military
as medals the authority
unquestioned
a silver ring bows the finger
(a silence) of carpet slippers
an old and unfashionable silence
in the era of the vote and Ruth's baby
       wherever he walks
       he flushes swarms of white butterflies
       and the bone china chatters
       he is a verb among meadow rue
the molecules lock
behind us and underneath a wind
oils the deeper dark
       he will never remember
       what he broke
we cannot return
neither in the silence
can we go forward
other than step by step
feeling with our hands and pinging like bats
for the echo

Early Frost

we turn toward each other anxiously tonight.
blighted shell beans
pole beans frozen in the postures of summer
green
tomatoes pulling the last pink from the sunset
dwarf melons regretting the shady weed
rain as cold as snow
stars as cold
as rain spelling the message of winter in September mud:
we listen
for the retreat
of a million monarchs

October

the noise of invisible geese
the barking behind black clouds

every autumn
today at noon
through the branches of another maple
I turn to the disappearing geese
with the sense of just
having missed something

I am another degree north
of where I started:
sun hits the tarragon
fifteen minutes later

the skin
around my cuticles,
on my heels, cracks; almanac of the shredding
autumn, the early winter

       the hammock fills with leaves
       a curl of pubic hair stiffens in the soap
       his heartbeat struggles inside my shoulder blade
       green flies and black flies nestle in black blood

you remember the instant
that the steer feeding at the bucket of grain
was next
the steer buckled in the attitude
of prayer
flies like scapulars around his neck

the skin laid out in the weak sun
tiny muscles twitching on the surface

October
again
every autumn
today
at noon
invisible geese behind black clouds

44

A Multiplicity of White Things

to walk
in the birch woods
without the insistence of autumn, after
hunting season

the breast of the African goose, neck
of the Indian Runner drake
green oil on white wick

winter pausing
on the hill where the old well fills with ground water

milkweed frozen in the pod

the step I take onto iced mud
by the beaver pond
certain it will break in the shallow of November

we remark
on the whiteness of birches
and goose-necks

and the melting and thawing
and surprising whiteness
of things

November

closer to the static level,
I watch a week pass aimlessly:
a green pick-up, brown station wagon,
an out-of-state car exploding with hunters, a dog
on his way home: out the window: against the sea heave
of the hills

the teapot is always full
the well inexhaustible and free of sulphur
Orion rises to the brim

Great Grey Owl

for Roberta

visited, simultaneously, the dreams of three
of us, accompanied by the death rattle
of a guinea hen, the silence of three
guinea hens under the abandoned porch; visited
its silence on our
attempts to speak
to each other

our tracks freeze
overnight, legible
even to the indifferent hunter

beware the creature
which climbs trees, eats
the most secret eggs

Raw Honey

the simple things

    the death of a dog
    a cat-killed bluejay

    the temperature of feet
    at night

    money

    whether
    a spark plug ignites
    on a grey morning, freezing rain

the first instinct is to turn away
still
the cousins of the bluejay continue
to crowd the swinging feeder
in necessary procession

and we get out of bed
every morning
for some reason

INTERSTATE

THE GEOGRAPHY: an itemization
in which chairs are lost
a lamp acquired for this new table
the plants at the window growing in every new house
rooted in pots and portable: requires
moon maps,
a recognition of constellations, a cross-indexed file
of the recipes we cook in each other's kitchens,
a flexible notion of time and direction,
the distance between exits
Food Fuel Lodging
an understanding of physics — the telephone
as emergency vehicle — and music

specifically

the arrangement of seeds
in the sunflower
and pine cones

you make
the irrational proportion
you then make
most works of art

the form occurs repeatedly
as a function of growth in plants and animals
the ratio occurs in the spirals
of the chambered nautilus
and Interstate 95

failing to make sense of these days
we repeat
patterns
like an old quilt

* * * * * * * * * * * * *

the letter from Jane in Oxford, Cynthia in the
yellow autumn of Taos, Ruth fretting:
　　'it's begun to rain
　　there will be green again but I miss the fall,
　　the barking anxiety of northern winter'
we can't identify
where it was we left

dear Sheri: I cannot imagine the Bronx. What are you doing
in the Bronx?

we are encysted
in shiny cocoons
averaging so many miles per gallon
collecting windshield stickers

we are the postcards of our generation/we are a forwarding
address
our speech is clipped, hurried
and the grocer just begins to know us

　　　　　　* * * * * * * * * * * * * *

no township or railroad crossing
to follow this road back to

this road was never widened
accommodates nothing

coons die violently
as I move smoothly from radio band to Cincinnati

now my body grows more beautiful
spare and polished
economical as a Shaker chair

lacking billboards, there is no cultural information
just trees
and blasted rocks: vertical maps

St Christopher is no longer a saint

watching the white dashes I remember
pressing my fingers into the oozing tar on the roads
in summer, the sound of cracking cement
under bicycle wheels

* * * * * * * * * * * * *

the old, pocked station smelling like piss
that's where you started from,
that's where you got a shoeshine from the huge shoeshine man
or gum or a fan mag

a place to write on the wall
make moustaches on the show posters

listen for the click of your high heels late in the evening;
head for the light at the end of the tunnel

  I-95 straight through Rye
thundering north
louder at night than a winter storm
no stops: feeding on and off ramps

I watch the train go by from a car window
fumbling in my pocket for exact change

* * * * * * * * * * * * *

I-495 avoids Boston
starts up the tiny NH coast another road

THERE ARE NO SERVICES ON THIS ROAD

the sand is crusty and salt whips off the rocks
at Hampton Beach
empty tide pools
footprints that remain like a fingerprint when dough has risen
the closest I come
to permanence

I carry you with me reluctantly
inside old books
in the prints at the corners of my eyes
in the pout of my son's mouth

            this death
            is organic: life's mulch: dead
            love

starting out
late at night knowing simply
that I will avoid Boston

* * * * * * * * * * * * *

out of gas
along the sinews of empire
somewhere between White River Junction
and Concord:

the car radio runs on lunar energy
playing continuous music of the spheres

the shades of hit-and-run animal victims rise
off the shoulders of the road   animals
long extinct:
does with old shoulder wounds
unborn fawns
possums with their tails curled around silver bumpers
raccoons with radiator grilles for faces
millions of butterflies, mosquitoes, ladybugs
preserved in radial perfection like ferns in shale

bits of paper emblazoned with golden arches blow in the grass
growing in the cracks in the pavement   the battery fills
with rainwater
constellations of diatoms speed through plankton night,
returning more darkness to the sky   mushrooms
come and go on the carpet
voles nest in the backseat and consume it

the stationary car   the stopped wave

we hunt for missing parts of our bodies
a feathered pouch lies beside the car
containing fingernail parings and baby teeth

* * * * * * * * * * * *

snow fattens the highway
the rivers are waiting to melt
never have we heard such silences

* * * * * * * * * * * * *

ice has locked the steering mechanism
glare ice locks the pavement in black.
alert,
I watch myself barrel north in the rear view mirror,
watch the mountains widening

behind the wheel, I believe
I am in control
I make the road diminish behind me,
make it disappear into a point
not unlike a tail light
red and fixed

* * * * * * * * * * * *

Leaving Ithaca: Buttermilk Falls
or the deep pool in Six Mile Creek where I swam,
shedding a day of late spring indoors
                         with my shirt and jeans,
squatted naked on the warm rocks with a few quiet friends;

leaving with my children north to Toronto
(north on I-89
west on 90 to Buffalo and across an international boundary
where even the names of the hamburger stands don't change):

three of us and our essentials
                         tape recorder full of music
                         2000 baseball trading cards
                         hiking boots and sweaters
                         typewriter
you learn
what to carry with you
                  now we are just three of the hundreds
on our way towards the Calgary Stampede   reluctant,
excited, fragile

aboard CNRR coach
settled and moving
out of Toronto, I imagine
hands at every smudged window
knocking for my attention
writing desperate messages on the dusty glass
"Don't go! It's the same
everywhere!"

                         monarch butterflies counting
                                 the distance
                         in short meter
                         from phone pole to pole until
                         they speed by too fast

55

north by Georgian Bay turning dark . . . . . Sudbury
west
to the Soo

                          we sleep sitting up
                          slumping on each other
Thunder Bay . . .
                 people
get off there
giving us more room
                          Thunder Bay: titles off library books
                          I used to read—magic beyond the
                          reality of smokestacks
Kenora . . . irish fog rising off the lakes
look way out the train window and see the end of the train
emerging from a forest, the engine ahead turning through
a forest

Manitoba-Saskatchewan . . . Winnipeg at midnight, like any
station at midnight: a rush for Hershey bars and magazines.
Standing on one foot, then the other wondering about
Winnipeg
            or
                 Regina, Moose Jaw, Swift Current
morning approaching Medicine Hat, Alberta
(meanwhile we pass the time train-fashion, eating and visiting,
walking like sailors)

Crossed the whole continent carrying the children
like saddlebags
                      when I dashed off the train for fresh bread
                      and cheese
                      they hung out the window yelling
                      as the conductor announced the minutes
                      till departure   schooled in departures,
                      we adapt to counting backwards

Calgary, Alberta, CANADA
                              south on Rt 2 by car to Fort McLeod
                              west on Rt 3 over Crow's Nest Pass.
                              (B.C.) to Fernie
(stopping for a few minutes at the Frank Slide, marvelling
where all these rocks came from
                              so fast
what it takes to bury a town
                              instantly)

TO: my next sister's home   FROM: Ithaca, Buttermilk Falls and
the deep pool in Six Mile Creek where I swam, shedding a day
of late, indoor spring with my shirt and jeans, squatting
naked with a few
quiet friends.

TO: Anny, my next sister   FROM: Ithaca, Buttermilk Falls,
a marriage of ten years

we make space for each other, pushing aside
a half-finished peanut butter and jelly sandwich,
a pile of newspaper. We make
idle conversation, layer on layer
travelling the miles of Interstate, the years of exits,
birthdays, children's birthdays

To Anny for a month in the Canadian Rockies
(the sky is a foggy weight belt on the Three Sisters, rain
like a mud boot on the valley, the bush is rain
and river)

                              Tango fell in love with me and I
                              fell in love with his
horses
salt lick
bighorn sheep

when you move around a lot you mistake sentiment
for home

57

mistake jealousy for love
separation for love
habit for love
children for love

Dear Anny:
                                    (and we write disjointed letters to each other

                    * * * * * * * * * * * *

We live with our mistakes
for 17 miles
to the next exit
the silence between us brims easily to anger

each headlight cuts the fog at a different angle
the thin clouds arrange themselves against a giant moon
in the image of a fish skeleton
                                    staying awake
fighting back: the temptation to sleep
Gethsemane
knowing it will begin again in the morning, craving
sleep's healing deception

the missed exit another accident
in the perpetual accident of our lives
together

REST AREA
in which
          (clean, machined, 24 hr)
I might
at another time
rest

                    * * * * * * * * * * * *

* * * * * * * * * * * * *

the sails strain out from the bent mast
kelp drifts on sea-soil, the salt
dries into maps on my arms

Hereschoff is dead
the S boat belongs to someone else
I walk by the edge of the highway   my hair
stiff with salt, bare footed
dragging shreds of seaweed and frayed rope,
a dry anchor
looking among the chicory for soil in which to plant them

* * * * * * * * * * * * *

Time is distorted the way it is
on days when winter moves through the intestines
raining in weepy spasms

I shuttle back and forth over the same bridge
on the same dime

My eyes are too tired to hold the road
I sleep fitfully in a Savarin parking lot dreaming
that pieces of my life are pulling away
like trucks

* * * * * * * * * * * * *

note from Colette sitting bare-assed on a wet towel in NYC
and Susan's going to Esalen   Sheri's leaving
the Bronx
            another year
most of the ties loosen like shoelaces, drag
along the ground
                        develop knots and catch in bicycle wheels

                    * * * * * * * * * * * *

letters home
 . . .we went up in the mountains and we found silver ore
and other rocks and bullit shells . . . we are having a ball . . .
 . . . guess what — by mistake I put my hand on a cactus and
guess what — I came up with *20* quills in my hand. But luckely
I was smart enough to get them out with a *nail clippers*
and also I fixed my glove all by myself!

the goat cries quietly and paces the length of his tether
the duck is missing
the goose sat on her eggs until they rotted
the first time we talked about divorce
in the south
when the children were babies:
                        you take this one
                        and I'll take that one
                        and I'll be in Scotland afore ye

                    * * * * * * * * * * * *

and what is spoken remains
in the synapses
the spaces
        between corn hills
        between cars on the highway
        between conversations, sentences, words
            or two people in the same bed
the electricity fails for an instant
a correspondent stops writing

* * * * * * * * * * * *

children travel best at night
sleep through the NJ Turnpike
through the detours and silent construction
through the night
smells and neon
around pink cities under
pale pink and yellow skies: the semidark
of the eastcoast
sleep curled
against cracked windows
the lights of tollbooths and truckstops flicker on their faces
REM of night landscape
that the driver
passes through

* * * * * * * * * * * *

Saul brings news of the West Side Highway:
they will remake the curving, pitted
road-to-the-ships
road-out-of-town
road that was always
a road from which: New Jersey and bridges and the huge Hudson

into an Interstate

what will become of the arched streetlights
and the Mobil station made of fieldstone?

* * * * * * * * * * * *
61

this summer
mosquitos breed
in the standing water
                    I have not moved in a year

am attracting ladybugs and butterflies

this summer I am lettuce
and snow peas scaling chickenwire like pale soldiers
a goose sitting on empty eggs
I have become magically old; I am a rocking chair and a lap robe

                * * * * * * * * * * * * *

the woman who cut her hair
moved a long distance
in thirty miles and ten days

some moves might as well be across countries
might as well indicate
new tongues, new
mouths
different flowers or
the absence of horses beside a junked car
an ocean and foghorn
where there was
a field of heavy goldenrod

is there any point
on the road
on which
you abandon
it all
where crying or laying your clipped head on the horn
or tying a white handerchief to the doorhandle
would summon
help

remember: you
are simply another
change-of-address   forget
that
and you will lose the power
of speech
in your hand

                    * * * * * * * * * * * *

                                    for Peggy

country/western sister
in Moscow, IDAHO dealing
trees   monocots, etc.
moving long distance in a Capri house w/tapedeck

climbed trees
drank treeblood
found
her secret place in the crotch of some
dying elm

                    * * * * * * * * * * * *

the street of schools
the street of the fishing cat
the street of the innocents
the square of the risen bread
the street of kites and ducklings

maple ave
state street
front street

                            we are not within walking
                            distance

                    * * * * * * * * * * * *

now it's my mother
who's moving

                  she worries for me in her dreams

moving! it must be
like ripping
the tree-climbing tree
out of the ground in winter: she may take
all of her land with her
held together by roots

                a piece of the ground
                and a piece of the frozen sky

when my mother hits the road
with her remaining children and little left
of her former life,

                I stay up late
                waiting for a phone call
                saying she's arrived

                    safely, my
                    daughter

    * * * * * * * * * * * *

you imagined the lover
I will never be I am

so sorry

tripping on the hem of it
falling backward
into the bottomless apology I am
so sorry:

like that
the fog shreds the edges of the horned moon
and yesterday's sharp snowfall

the road home
is a short memory
I reinvent ahead of the low beams

* * * * * * * * * * * * *

the completion of the stretch
between here and the border
is in doubt

I am camped in the shadow of the earth
movers

* * * * * * * * * * * * *